ST

Greater Than a Tourist E

s

I think the series is wonderful and beneficial for tourists to get information before visiting the city.

-Seckin Zumbul, Izmir Turkey

I am a world traveler who has read many trip guides but this one really made a difference for me. I would call it a heartfelt creation of a local guide expert instead of just a guide.

-Susy, Isla Holbox, Mexico

New to the area like me, this is a must have!

-Joe, Bloomington, USA

This is a good series that gets down to it when looking for things to do at your destination without having to read a novel for just a few ideas.

-Rachel, Monterey, USA

Good information to have to plan my trip to this destination.

-Pennie Farrell, Mexico

Aptly titled, you won't just be a tourist after reading this book. You'll be greater than a tourist!

-Alan Warner, Grand Rapids, USA

Thank you for a fantastic book.

-Don, Philadelphia, USA

Jennifer Baines

Great ideas for a port day.

-Mary Martin USA

Even though I only have three days to spend in San Miguel in an upcoming visit, I will use the author's suggestions to guide some of my time there. An easy read - with chapters named to guide me in directions I want to go.

-Robert Catapano, USA

Great insights from a local perspective! Useful information and a very good value!

-Sarah, USA

This series provides an in-depth experience through the eyes of a local. Reading these series will help you to travel the city in with confidence and it'll make your journey a unique one.

-Andrew Teoh, Ipoh, Malaysia

Tourists can get an amazing "insider scoop" about a lot of places from all over the world. While reading, you can feel how much love the writer put in it.

-Vanja Živković, Sremski Karlovci, Serbia

GREATER THAN A TOURIST – CAMBRIDGE UNITED KINGDOM

50 Travel Tips from a Local

Jennifer Baines

Jennifer Baines

Cover designed by Ivana Stamenković
Cover images: https://pixabay.com/en/old-building-castle-cambridge-16707/

Greater Than a Tourist
Visit our website at www.GreaterThanaTourist.com

Lock Haven, PA

ISBN: 9781980645566

>TOURIST

50 TRAVEL TIPS FROM A LOCAL

Jennifer Baines

BOOK DESCRIPTION

Are you excited about planning your next trip?
Do you want to try something new?
Would you like some guidance from a local?

If you answered yes to any of these questions, then this Greater Than a Tourist book is for you.

Greater Than a Tourist – Cambridge, UK by Jennifer Baines offers the inside scope on the city of Cambridge in England. Most travel books tell you how to travel like a tourist. Although there is nothing wrong with that, as part of the Greater Than a Tourist series, this book will give you travel tips from someone who has lived at your next travel destination.

In these pages, you will discover advice that will help you throughout your stay. This book will not tell you exact addresses or store hours but instead will give you excitement and knowledge from a local that you may not find in other smaller print travel books.

Travel like a local. Slow down, stay in one place, and get to know the people and the culture. By the time you finish this book, you will be eager and prepared to travel to your next destination.

Jennifer Baines

TABLE OF CONTENTS

DEDICATION

This book is dedicated to my late father, who - along with my mother - brought me to live in this fascinating and beautiful city.

Thanks, Dad, for all the adventures!

Jennifer Baines

ABOUT THE AUTHOR

Jennifer Baines has lived in Cambridge since her parents moved back to the UK from her birthplace in Sydney, Australia, when she was two years old. She studied at the University of Lincoln, where she also met her husband.

After working as a magazine Production Editor, Jennifer took time off to enjoy being a mum to her two boys, but her love of travel has never left her and now it is a passion she enjoys sharing with her family. Together, they have traveled extensively, exploring new places and creating memories to last a lifetime.

She now spends her time working in the adult learning department of her local college, freelance writing and editing, and blogging about family travel.

For Jennifer, every day is the chance for another adventure and she hopes to inspire the same love of travel in others. This book is a chance for her to divulge some of her favourite things about her hometown of Cambridge and explain why it will always have a special place in her heart.

Jennifer Baines

HOW TO USE THIS BOOK

The Greater Than a Tourist book series was written by someone who has lived in an area for over three months. The goal of this book is to help travelers either dream or experience different locations by providing opinions from a local. The author has made suggestions based on their own experiences. Please do your own research before traveling to the area in case the suggested places are unavailable.

Jennifer Baines

FROM THE PUBLISHER

Traveling can be one of the most important parts of a person's life. The anticipation and memories that you have are some of the best. As a publisher of the Greater Than a Tourist book series, as well as the popular 50 Things to Know book series, we strive to help you learn about new places, spark your imagination, and inspire you. Wherever you are and whatever you do I wish you safe, fun, and inspiring travel.

Lisa Rusczyk Ed. D.
CZYK Publishing

Jennifer Baines

OUR STORY

Traveling is a passion of the "Greater than a Tourist" series creator. Lisa studied abroad in college, and for their honeymoon Lisa and her husband toured Europe. During her travels to Malta, an older man tried to give her some advice based on his own experience living on the island since he was a young boy. She was not sure if she should talk to the stranger but was interested in his advice. When traveling to some places she was wary to talk to locals because she was afraid that they weren't being genuine. Through her travels, Lisa learned how much locals had to share with tourists. Lisa created the "Greater Than a Tourist" book series to help connect people with locals. A topic that locals are very passionate about sharing.

Jennifer Baines

WELCOME TO > TOURIST

Jennifer Baines

INTRODUCTION

"Cambridge is one of the best universities in the world, especially in my field."

\- Stephen Hawking

For nearly 30 years I have lived in Cambridge, England, a city bursting at the seams with historic character and a place of immense academic achievement, where some of the greatest influential thinkers and creative minds from the last 500 years have lived and learned. It is also a delightful mix of urban and country, with cows grazing on public greens and numerous tranquil walks to be found amid the hustle and bustle of city life.

Although steeped in tradition, Cambridge still manages to be thoroughly modern. Chock-full of world-class shopping and leisure activities, it plays host to a variety of festivals throughout the year.

I have found Cambridge to be a city for all seasons, with something for everyone, of all ages. It is a place where culture and quirkiness combine to create the perfect blend of good old-fashioned, thoroughly British fun.

1. Take a Self-Guided Tour of the University

You can't come to Cambridge and not see the famous University - it's all around! People often make the mistake of thinking before their visit that the University is one specific building, but there are actually 31 colleges in total. The oldest, Peterhouse, was established in 1284. While most of them let visitors enter for free, some charge a small fee and it is best to check the individual college's website in case of closure to the public during exams.

You don't have to get inside the colleges to appreciate their architecture and most are within easy walking distance of each other. Perhaps the most famous is King's College, facing out onto historic King's Parade. This is the one they always seem to feature on TV or in films and it is certainly photogenic. Equally prestigious is Trinity college, whose alumni include physicist Sir Isaac Newton, poet Lord Byron and novelist A. A. Milne.

Countless influential figures in the fields of mathematics, science, politics, law and philosophy have walked the halls of these temples of research and learning. Here are just a few of the famous people who went to Cambridge University:

Oliver Cromwell, Sidney Sussex College, 1617
Charles Darwin, Christ's College, 1831
Stephen Hawking, Trinity Hall College, 1965
Charles, Prince of Wales, Trinity College, 1970
Emma Thompson, actress, Newnham College, 1980

2. Immerse Yourself in Museums

If museums are your thing, you certainly have your pick of them here! The University of Cambridge has eight, most of which are within walking distance from the city centre. They run various events throughout the year, one of the most popular being Twilight at the Museums.

Fitzwilliam Museum - You can't miss it, with its big white columns and neo-classic architecture. Just a stone's throw from King's College, it houses art and antiquities, including Ancient Greek, Roman and Egyptian collections.

Kettle's Yard - A house and gallery of contemporary and modern art. The permanent collection was established by former resident Jim Ede (who worked as a curator at London's Tate Gallery) and his wife, Helen.

Museum of Archaeology and Anthropology - These collections span more than two million years of human history, including art, sculptures and artefacts from every continent.

Museum of Classical Archaeology - It has one of the largest plaster cast collections in the world, including many recognisable ancient Greek and Roman sculptures.

Museum of Zoology - Home to various displays about evolution and specimens relating to animals from all over the world.

The Polar Museum - Part of the Scott Polar Research Institute, with intriguing exhibitions about the polar regions and expeditions led by Captain Scott and other explorers.

Sedgwick Museum of Earth Sciences - The oldest of the University's museums, housing over two million fossils, rocks and minerals.

Whipple Museum of the History of Science - Lots of science-related instruments and apparatus are housed here, some dating back to medieval times.

3. Picnic in a City Park

Much of Cambridge's appeal lies in its plentiful parks and green spaces. You would be hard-pressed to find another city where the surrounding countryside merges so beautifully with its busy streets. Even the cows have found their way into the centre! The parks come alive with colourful flowers in spring and summer, and you don't have to go far to find the perfect picnic spot.

Jesus Green - next to Jesus College - is my favourite. Tree-lined avenues provide plenty of shade and acres of grass for playing ball games, and there is a refreshment kiosk where you can buy drinks and ice creams. I like to come here to feed ducks with the kids and watch narrowboats on the river. There is also a great playground.

Midsummer Common is just over the road from Jesus Green and is where they hold the annual city fair. Many of the college rowing clubs have their boat houses on the opposite bank and it's fun to watch the teams practise.

In the very centre of town, just up from the main shopping area on Regent Street, is Parker's Piece, a wide open common regarded by many to be the birthplace of the rules of football. A small plaque on a tree in the corner commemorates the students who established a common set of rules for the game here in the 1800s. In winter, there is an open-air ice rink and Santa's grotto on Parker's Piece dubbed 'The North Pole', which always gets me in the festive mood.

On the other side of the bus station, Christ's Pieces are a great little oasis if you're looking for a pit stop between the two main shopping areas of the Grand Arcade and Grafton Centre. There are plenty of grassy areas to eat lunch, plus tennis courts and a bowling green.

Sheep's Green and Coe Fen make up a nature reserve of low-lying meadowlands within walking distance from the city centre. This area is mainly used as grazing land for cattle, but you can find a bench among the willow trees to sit and eat your sandwiches. Head further along the path towards the Mill and Granta pubs and you'll hit upon a popular place for picnickers and drinkers alike.

Over the bridge from Coe Fen, you'll come to Lamma's Land, which is a fantastic place to take the kids on a sunny day. The park has a huge playground with enough equipment to keep both young and older kids happy, as well as a large paddling pool and tennis courts. Just remember to pack their swimming cossies and some sunscreen - it can get quite hot here in summer!

4. Shop Until You Drop

Cambridge's bustling city centre is fairly compact, meaning most of the main shopping areas are within walking distance of each other. A few years ago, the indoor Grand Arcade shopping mall was added to what locals still refer to as 'Lion Yard'. There are more than 60 stores here offering a good selection of brands and high street names, as well as a large John Lewis department store.

Just outside is the pedestrianized shopping street of Petty Cury. In fact, the whole area around Sidney Street and Market Street provides an exciting mix of high street and designer labels.

A short walk from St Andrews Street across Christ's Pieces brings you to Fitzroy Street and the undercover Grafton Centre. The shops here are mainly affordable high street names, but take a stroll down adjacent Burleigh Street and you will find independent specialist stores as well as several charity shops.

For quirky and chic shops, head back towards the colleges: Rose Crescent for beauty and pampering; Trinity Street for boutiques and pretty homewares; Bridge Street for jewellery, pottery and health stores; and King's Parade for fine art galleries and camera-related equipment. Cambridge's cobbled Market Square sells everything from vintage clothing to vegetables and is open every day of the week. All Saints Garden, off Trinity Street, holds an art and craft market every Saturday. For souvenirs, I would recommend the tourist information centre at the Guildhall, The Little Gift Shop On The Corner in Rose Crescent, Typically British on Bridge Street and Jacks On Trinity on Trinity Street.

The Cambridge Cheese Company in All Saints Passage is a hidden gem for lovers of fine artisan foods.

5. Spend a lazy day on the River Cam

The best way to get views of the famous college 'Backs' is to glide along the River Cam in a traditional punt.

Punting companies such as Scudamore's and Magdalene Bridge Punts offer guided tours from Quayside and Granta Place taking in the city's various landmarks, or you can hire one yourself. It's fairly easy once you get the hang of it, and you can stick with town or head out towards Grantchester Meadows.

Getting to grips with the steering and the sheer entertainment of watching others do the same makes the whole experience a lot of fun. Bring a picnic and make a day of it!

How to punt:

- Stand on the rear deck, legs slightly apart for stability.

- Put the pole in the water to one side of the boat.

- Push down against the riverbed with the pole until the punt is moving.

- Steer by trailing the pole in the water behind you, similar to using a rudder.

- Whatever you do, don't drop the pole!

6. Stop for Afternoon Tea

"There are few hours in life more agreeable than the hour dedicated to the ceremony known as afternoon tea."

- Henry James, The Portrait of a Lady

Ah, the grand old British tradition of afternoon tea! If you've never had it, you really should. Well-known lyrics from the old musical Come Out of the Pantry claim that "At half-past three, everything stops for tea." These days, it's a bit of a luxury we Brits reserve for special occasions, but it's a must for tourists!

The perfect spread consists of finger sandwiches, scones served with clotted cream and jam, a selection of cakes and pastries, and pots of tea poured into dainty teacups on saucers. Go for a 'Champagne tea' and you'll get a glass of fizz too.

Cambridge has plenty of tearooms and one of the best is the Orchard Tea Garden at Grantchester, which started in 1897 when a group of students asked the owner of Orchard House if she would serve them tea and cakes beneath the fruit trees. The ritual stuck and ever since people have enjoyed afternoon tea here, including famous names like Alan Turing, Virginia Woolf, Bertrand Russell and Rupert Brooke. This is a place which, in the words of the latter, remains "forever England". They serve a great range of tea and it is very relaxing to sit in the deckchairs soaking up the sun while enjoying a good cuppa. Harriet's Tearoom, located on Green Street in the city centre, has friendly staff plus a varied and tasty menu. On some afternoons they even have a pianist playing.

Further afield, as part of a day trip to the town of Ely, I highly recommend the Almonry Tearoom overlooking the gardens of Ely Cathedral. It is a really peaceful place and they have a great selection of cakes. Alternatively, down by the river at Ely there is another little gem called Peacocks, which is wonderfully quaint and offers pretty views of the Great Ouse and Ely marina.

If I had to choose, my top tearoom pick would be the River Terrace Café at nearby St Ives. It is very family-friendly, you can sit outside right next to the river and the fruit scones are absolutely delicious.

7. Get the best view of the City

Cambridge, like most of the county of Cambridgeshire, is flat. Really flat. If you want a birds-eye view of the city, there is only really one place to go: the tower at Great St Mary's Church. Pay a small fee to take the spiral staircase up 123 steps for a panoramic view of the colleges and Market Hill. It's a good way to get your bearings when you first arrive.

As an alternative, you could climb Castle Hill, a grassy mound which was originally an Iron Age hill fort and later a Roman town named Duroliponte. It's pretty much the only hill around here and is opposite the County Council's HQ. People often have their wedding photos taken on it after marrying at the registry office. Stand at the top on a clear day and you can see all the way to Ely Cathedral.

8. Listen to the King's College Choir

In 1441, King Henry VI founded King's College in Cambridge, and the angelic voices of the King's College Choir have rung out from its chapel ever since. Famous the world over, the Choir is the ultimate example of English choral tradition, with millions tuning in every Christmas Eve to listen to their Festival of Nine Lessons and Carols, broadcast annually since 1931.

Charles Darwin liked their singing so much he even hired them to sing in his rooms while he was at Christ's College, and I don't blame him because there is nothing better than hearing the Choir live. They have sung at major UK concert halls and festivals, as well as touring abroad, but listening to them sing evensong in their own chapel is a truly special experience.

Choral services are held at 5.30pm from Monday to Saturday, and at 10.30am and 3.30pm on Sunday. You don't need to purchase a ticket, but it is best to get there at least 30 minutes before, as there are often queues. Be aware also that the full choir sing on Tuesday, Thursday, Friday, Saturday and Sunday. Monday evensong is sung by King's College's mixed voice choir and Wednesday evensong is sung by the men's voices only.

9. Have a pint in the pub where DNA was Announced

All the best ideas start with a bevvie or two, and The Eagle pub on Bene't Street is where Francis Crick and James Watson first announced their discovery of 'the secret of life' in 1953. There's even a plaque outside to commemorate it and they serve a special 'DNA' bitter at the bar.

One of the pub's most interesting historical features is its RAF bar, a regular haunt for airmen during the Second World War. Their graffiti can still be seen on its ceiling.

If you're feeling peckish, this former 17th century coaching inn does a mean fish & chips, but make sure you leave room for pudding.

Oh, and for those with an interest in the supernatural, The Eagle is supposedly haunted by the ghost of a little boy (or young barmaid, depending on who is telling it) who perished in a fire here centuries ago.

10. Catch a Movie at the Film Festival

The Cambridge Film Festival, which takes place each October, is run by the charity Cambridge Film Trust, screening old movies as well as new ones. Some major films have had their UK premiere here, including Woody Allen's Crimes and Misdemeanours, Quentin Tarantino's Reservoir Dogs and Disney's Pirates of the Caribbean: The Curse of the Black Pearl.

Over the years, the Film Festival has showcased a diverse range of films, not just from emerging talent in the UK but from around the world. Screenings take place at various venues throughout the city, including the Arts Picturehouse on St Andrew's Street, and there are also outdoor screenings at Grantchester Meadows and Jesus Green. Tickets can be booked online or at the Arts Picturehouse.

11. Admire Cambridge's Architecture

To find out more about Cambridge's historical buildings and landmarks, you could book an official guided walking tour, but most of the highlights are easy to find yourself. Aside from the magnificent architecture of the colleges, there are several features worth looking out for.

Connected to President's Lodge, the oldest building on the river, is the Queen's College bridge, which locals refer to as the 'Mathematical Bridge'. Contrary to what the guides will tell you, it was not built by Sir Isaac Newton, but was designed by carpenter William Etheridge and built by James Essex the Younger in 1749. It has an interesting self-supporting structure.

Located at St John's College is the Bridge of Sighs. It was named after the famous bridge in Venice, but the only similarity between the two seems to be that they are both covered. Cambridge's neo-gothic version is best viewed from a river punt.

On the corner of Bene't Street and Trumpington Street, on the outside of the Taylor Library at Corpus Christi College, there is a distinctive sculptural clock set into the wall. Invented and designed by

Dr John C Taylor OBE FREng, it gives the time without hands or numbers, using three LED rings, which show hours, minutes and seconds reading from the innermost ring. The design features a monster - a 'chronophage', meaning time-eater - and the latin inscription mundus transit et concupiscentia eius underneath, which means 'the world and its desires pass away'.

The Church of the Holy Sepulchre - or Round Church - is Cambridge's second oldest building. Located on Bridge Street, it was built in the Norman style in the 12th century and is one of only four round churches in England. It is now a visitor centre where you can learn about the history of Cambridge and Christianity's impact upon England.

King's College Chapel is a stunning example of late medieval architecture and has the largest fan vaulted ceiling in the world, as well as magnificent stained-glass windows.

The oldest building in Cambridge is St Bene't's Church, situated on Bene't Street. Parts of the church, including the tower and the magnificent carved archway, are Anglo-Saxon.

A stone's throw from the Abbey Stadium on Newmarket Road, you could easily miss the Leper Chapel if you weren't looking for it. Also known as the Chapel of St Mary Magdalene, it dates back to the 12th century and was part of an isolation hospital for sufferers of leprosy.

The University's Senate House is a beautiful example of neo-classical architecture. Built in the 18th century, these days it is used mainly for graduation ceremonies.

If you walk down Magdalene Street or Bridge Street, you may wonder (as I did) why there are tiny flowers set into the pavement here. There are 600 of them in total and, as a plaque on the wall on the corner of Magdalene Street and Chesterton Lane explains, they are part of a public art project. They link to architectural flowers that decorate the surrounding University buildings and railings.

12. All the fun of the Fairs

The tradition of fairs in the UK goes back centuries and Cambridge's Midsummer Fair in June is one of the oldest, being in its 807th year. With rides, candyfloss and hot-dogs, it's all you could want from a funfair and more, with a great setting on Midsummer Common near the city centre.

Strawberry Fair is also held on Midsummer Common, on the first Saturday of June, and is a popular one-day festival celebrating music, arts and crafts. With an eclectic range of entertainment and live music, this not-for-profit fair run by volunteers has a reputation for being a bit 'hippy-ish', which many would say is part of its charm.

The historic Michaelmas Fair in October has been coming to the nearby town of St Ives since the 14th century and has lots of rides and stalls running all through the market square and main shopping street. Come on opening night and you will see the mayor handing out pennies, as is tradition.

13. Relax in the Botanic Garden

As well as eight museums, Cambridge University boasts its very own botanical gardens with more than 8000 plant species from around the world. These beautifully landscaped gardens are an important academic resource, as well as a great place to relax and escape from busy city life. It is not uncommon to see artists here with their easels, which is understandable.

With 40 acres to explore, including a lake, scented garden, rose garden, bee borders and glasshouses, the Botanic Garden has seasonal trails to ensure visitors can enjoy it all year round. Squirrels, foxes, badgers, muntjac deer, water voles, frogs, grass snakes, butterflies and numerous birds and other insects have made a home for themselves here.

At Woolsthorpe Manor in Lincolnshire there is an apple tree which is said to have been the tree that inspired Sir Isaac Newton's theory of gravity. A descendant of this tree by propagation grows in the lawn here at the Botanic Garden.

There is an entrance fee, but admission is free for under 16s. Be sure to stop by the café for a coffee and some delicious homemade cake.

14. Explore the Darker side of Cambridge

In a city as old as Cambridge, it's not surprising to hear that some of its buildings are haunted.

Corpus Christi College is one of the most haunted, supposedly by the ghost of Dr Henry Butts, a former master who hung himself from the door of the Master's Lodge. A failed exorcism was attempted by students at the college in 1904. In 1667, master's daughter Elizabeth Spencer threw herself from the roof here after her lover suffocated whilst hiding in a closet, and the pair are allegedly sighted at the college every Christmas Eve.

You can book a ghost tour for a spine-tingling journey through the city's macabre past, but just how real are these ghosts? That is a matter of opinion, of course, but it's worth keeping in mind that Cambridge is also the home of the world's oldest ghost club, which was started by a group of Trinity College students including Charles Dickens. It is claimed that past members continued to communicate with the group long after their deaths. Spooky or what?!

15. Listen to Live Music Across the City

"Music is a moral law. It gives soul to the universe, wings to the mind, flight to the imagination…" - Plato

Being less than an hour's train ride from London, Cambridge is conveniently situated for major concert arenas like the O2 and Wembley, but if you're looking for live music in the city itself there are plenty of venues to choose from, both big and small.

The Corn Exchange, just up from the market, is where to go for bigger names. It has a varied line-up - from rock, pop and folk artists to orchestral performances - and is the largest entertainment venue in the area.

Back in the '90s, The Junction was the place to be on a Saturday night and I spent many late-night hours here in my teens boogieing with friends. These days, the venue sits on the edge of the Clifton Way Cambridge Leisure Park near the railway station, boasting a diverse range of music from well-known and up-and-coming talent. The Junction's smaller size gives it a more intimate setting.

If you're looking for music of a more classical kind, the West Road Concert Hall is a good bet. As part of the University's Faculty of Music, this venue has superb acoustics and holds regular orchestral concerts.

As Cambridge is a university town, it's no surprise that some of the best places to find live music here are at pubs. The Portland Arms on the corner of Chesterton Road and Victoria Road offers real ales and live music in a traditional 1930s pub. They are an incredibly friendly bunch, welcoming up-and-coming artists of all genres from both the UK and abroad, and there is always a lively atmosphere.

The Cornerhouse pub on Newmarket Road also holds regular gigs by local and international bands, as well as acoustic nights and live jazz events.

The Earl of Beaconsfield on Mill Road is a thriving community pub with live music four nights a week, including acoustic jams and guest appearances from local talent.

16. Go on the Ultimate Riverside Ramble

Cambridge's riverside setting and architectural splendour make a walk along the Backs an attractive proposition at any time of year. This is an area of the city where several of the colleges back onto the River Cam, giving stunning views just right for a selfie!

If you fancy extending your walk, you can take the route all the way from the city centre through Coe Fen Nature Reserve and Sheep's Green to the picturesque village of Grantchester. This takes you through peaceful woodland and meadows. In the summer, the river is busy with punters and canoeists.

Grantchester itself was once home to the poet Rupert Brooke and further upstream is Byron's Pool, a nature reserve named after Lord Byron, who is rumoured to have swum at the weir pool here. The village is also the setting of British TV drama Grantchester, which was filmed on location using local residents as extras.

17. Sample a few Bevvies at the Beer Festival

One of the largest regional beer festivals in the UK, the Cambridge Beer Festival is held on Jesus Green at the end of May. It has been running since 1974, showcasing a huge range of local, national and international beers, both bottled and draft.

Run by volunteers as part of the Campaign for Real Ale (CAMRA), the festival attracts a huge number of visitors each year. Don't like beer? No worries! There are plenty of other tipples available, plus a great selection of fine cheeses, bread and other local produce.

18. Visit the Leisure Park for Family Fun

Museums and colleges are all very well and good, but sometimes you just want to have some fun. Keeping the whole family entertained can be tricky, so head on over to the Cambridge Leisure Park where there is something for everyone.

Located a short walk from the train station, this complex has a good selection of restaurants, plus a cinema, arcade games and ten-pin bowling. You can also hire one of their Sing Dizzy karaoke booths - great for a laugh!

Upstairs next to the cinema is Nines, a global buffet serving hundreds of dishes from around the world at a set price.

Just around the corner, on the Clifton Road Industrial Estate, you will find Clip 'n' Climb, a fantastic rock climbing centre with lots of different climbing challenges and a vertical drop slide.

19. Watch Shakespeare Outdoors

"All the world's a stage, and all the men and women merely players…" - William Shakespeare, As You Like It

There is no better way to enjoy a Shakespearean play than sitting in the open air on a warm summer's eve, sipping a glass of sparkling wine and munching on strawberries. If you are visiting Cambridge in July or August, the city's eight-week Shakespeare Festival is not to be missed.

You can take a picnic and enjoy live Elizabethan music as the Bard's much-loved works are performed in full period costume in a number of the colleges' private gardens. There are no special effects and there is no stage; just the plays being acted out around you, which makes it all the more magical. A Midsummer Night's Dream and Much Ado About Nothing are particular favourites of mine.

20. Go for a Swim - Indoors and Outdoors

If you fancy a dip or just want to splash around with the family, Parkside Pool opposite Parker's Piece in the city centre is the best place to go. There are three pools: a 25m, eight-lane pool; a teaching and diving pool with movable floor where they also hold family sessions; and a children's leisure pool with little waterfall slides. Parkside also has two flume rides, including one suitable for two people to ride.

The Abbey Leisure Complex on Whitehill Road just off Newmarket Road has a 25m pool with five lanes and a smaller teaching pool, plus an outdoor splashpad.

If the weather is fine, head to the historic lido by the river at Jesus Green. This outdoor pool is open to the public from May to September and has a sauna as well as lots of space for sunbathing.

All three of these pools are inexpensive and have good changing facilities.

21. Camp out at the Folk Festival

Every year in July, thousands flock to Cambridge's famous Folk Festival - one of the longest running in Europe - and it's no wonder why. Held in the grounds of Cherry Hinton Hall, the festival is laid-back, unpretentious and family-friendly, providing space for camping nearby and on-site entertainment for kids.

The line-up is always a brilliant mix of well-known artists and new talent, both local and international, offering much more than what you might consider to be traditional folk music. As part of the festival's commitment to showcasing what the next generation of musicians has to offer, there is a stage called The Den especially for artists under 30 years old and a dedicated Hub area for young musicians.

Cambridge Folk Festival takes place in an attractive riverside and woodland location with good facilities, less than 15 minutes from the city centre. Just be sure to get your tickets early, as the event does sell out quickly.

22. Venture into the Fens for Wildlife Spotting

To the north of the city lie the Cambridgeshire Fens, miles of very flat farmland that used to be part of a vast inland waterway system before the marshes were drained over several centuries. The resulting wetlands are a haven for birds and other wildlife.

There are a number of wetland nature reserves not far from the city and over the years I've spotted ducks, swans, geese, harriers, terns, grebes, lapwings, wigeons and starlings. The most impressive facilities are at the WWT (Wildfowl & Wetlands Trust) centre at Welney. Here you will find fenland exhibitions, art and craft activity stations, a heated hide and swan research station and a café. If you've got kids, make sure they pick up an explorer backpack from the gift shop.

Whilst there is plenty to discover all year round, the Winter Swan Spectacle is the most impressive time to come, when migrating flocks arrive daily and the reserve is teeming with birds. Be prepared, however, for the possibility of some of the footpaths being closed due to flooding.

Wicken Fen near Ely is another wonderful nature reserve, run by the National Trust. Over 9000 species have been recorded here and the reserve has nine different hides. I visited many times when I was younger on school trips, then later with kids of my own, and it's great for walks and family bike rides. The boardwalk trail provides access for all abilities, taking you past a historic windpump, and there is also a café and gift shop. You can book to wild camp here in open shelters and toast marshmallows over the fire pit, and there are various family activities on offer all year round. A favourite with my kids is the pond dipping.

If you're not bothered by a lack of facilities or you don't want to pay an entry fee, Fen Drayton Lakes is the ideal place for bird spotting. It used to be a sand and gravel quarry before it was flooded and now it attracts ducks, geese, swans and other waterbirds, as well as dragonflies and otters. Surrounded by meadows, it's good for walking, cycling or having a picnic, plus there are three open shelters and one hide for wildlife viewing

Tips for wildlife spotting:

- OK, so this might seem like an obvious one, but remember to bring your binoculars. And be patient!

- Don't wear bright colours - neutral colours are better for blending in. Be sure to wrap up well in autumn and winter with warm clothing and waterproofs.

- Early morning, dusk or late evening are the best times for wildlife spotting.

- Some centres have sightings books where people can record what they have seen. Check these out to get an idea of what species are around and don't forget to fill in your own sightings for that day.

- Consider purchasing a field guide to help you identify species. If you're not sure what something is, ask. Staff, volunteers and other wildlife enthusiasts are more than happy to help.

23. Enjoy a day at Newmarket Races

If you fancy a flutter, Newmarket Racecourse is known as the 'home of British horseracing', and is a fun and exciting day out. Flat races take place here at the Rowley Mile in spring and autumn or the Adnams July Course in summer.

There is something for everyone at Newmarket and your experience really depends on what type of ticket you purchase. If you opt for the family-friendly paddock enclosure, you'll find a play area, bouncy castles and face painting, but you won't have access to the restaurants and specialist views. Many people bring their own picnic and chairs to the paddock.

If there is a chance of rain or you want to be closer to the finish line, opt for the grandstand. There are also hospitality suites available to book for that extra special occasion.

The dress code is generally relaxed, unless you are in the Premier or Hospitality enclosures, but some events are more glam than others. Ladies Day in July, for example, is the height of sophisticated style and fashion.

Top tips:

- It is a good idea to visit to the parade ring before a race, as you get to see the runners before they head out onto the course. Look for a shiny coat, good muscle tone and alertness before placing your bet.

- For more about the history of British horseracing, visit the National Horseracing Museum at Palace House in Newmarket. They have a racehorse simulator to ride!

24. Visit Magnificent Ely Cathedral

Often referred to as the 'Ship of the Fens' due to it being visible for miles around in Cambridgeshire's flat landscape, Ely Cathedral is a stunning feat of architecture. Its nave is the third longest in the UK and its Octagon Tower is known worldwide as a masterpiece of engineering. Originally founded by Queen Etheldreda in 673, it was re-founded as a Benedictine monastery in 970, and over the centuries there have been various additions and restorations.

The Cathedral was the subject of many a school project when I was young and I simply cannot emphasise how atmospheric it is, especially if you are lucky enough to catch the boys' choir at evensong, which they perform every day of the week during British term time. It has been used as a filming location on numerous occasions, featuring in movies such as The King's Speech, Elizabeth: The Golden Age and The Other Boleyn Girl, as well as UK TV drama The Crown.

Other great features include the Lady Chapel, which is the largest of its kind in the UK, and the lawns and gardens that surround the Cathedral, giving fantastic views of its exterior.

You don't have to be religious to enjoy this place; just wander around and take in the unique atmosphere. If you get peckish, the Refectory Cafe serves delicious sausage rolls and other snacks.

25. Get Lost... in a Maze

Mazes - you either love 'em or you hate 'em. There are a few dotted around Cambridge and the surrounding area, some of which have historical importance, and I think they're great fun.

Not far from Cambridge, the market town of Saffron Walden has three mazes: a hedge maze at Bridge End Garden; a turf maze on the common in the middle of town; and a paved labyrinth in the Jubilee Garden bandstand. The turf maze here is the largest of its kind in the world and one of only eight surviving in England.

Between Cambridge and Huntingdon, the pretty village of Hilton has a turf maze at one end of its green, which was made in 1660 by a chap named William Sparrow. The monument at its centre commemorates him.

The aforementioned Ely Cathedral has its very own labyrinth on the tiles just inside the entrance which, if you follow it right to the end, takes you the same distance as the height of the ceiling above. There are no dead ends, but the twists and turns are apparently representative of the journey of life.

In the summer, maize mazes pop up all over the country and the closest one to Cambridge is at Milton. Farmer Rob and his maze team create a huge maze in a different pattern each year. There is also a field of fun for kids, filled with giant slides, go karts and tractor rides.

26. Take a trip to Historic St Ives

"Here are the most beautiful meadows on the banks of the River Ouse, that are to be seen in any part of England." -

Daniel Defoe

There are a number of interesting towns not far from Cambridge, but my favourite is the pretty market town of St Ives. You can drive or catch the guided bus here from the city centre. As well as quaint alleyways and historic buildings, St Ives has an attractive waterfront where a 15th century bridge spans the Great Ouse River, complete with its own chapel. Swans and riverboats meander up and down, and the view across the meadows is simply stunning.

St Ives has plenty of shops and cafes, plus a regular market on Mondays and Fridays. If you are looking for somewhere to eat lunch, the Golden Lion Hotel in the market square provides a varied and tasty menu in comfortable surroundings. The River Terrace Café next to the bridge is my choice for afternoon tea.

You can take a riverboat cruise from The Old Riverport quay or there are numerous enjoyable walking routes along the river to the villages of Hemingford Abbots, Houghton and Holywell. Up by All Saints Parish Church, you can access a boardwalk that will take you around Holt Island Nature Reserve (open April to September), which is a haven for wildlife.

Although the town in the old nursery rhyme riddle beginning, "As I was going to St Ives, I met a man with seven wives," is generally thought to be St Ives in Cornwall, some argue it actually refers to this St Ives.

27. Enjoy an Action-packed day at Duxford

During the First World War, Duxford was an airfield, then a fighter station in WW2. These days, it is the site of the Imperial War Museum, which hosts air shows throughout the year.

The two-day Flying Legends show takes place at the beginning of July, and the main Duxford Air Show is in early autumn and is themed. The shows are really impressive, with spitfires, bombers and jets roaring overhead, exciting parachute displays and vintage entertainment for those on the ground. The museum and hangars are free on air show days, so you can get up close to hundreds of aircraft and aviation objects.

As if all that wasn't exciting enough, IWM Duxford also offer flying experiences and lessons.

28. Have fun on the farm at Wimpole Hall Estate

Among the most interesting of England's historic buildings are its stately homes. Rich in heritage and culture, many of these country estates have been preserved by the National Trust and boast beautifully landscaped gardens. Just eight miles out of Cambridge, Wimpole Hall is one of these.

When I was growing up, Wimpole was a family favourite for a day out, and not an awful lot has changed over the years, which is part of its appeal. It is a working estate with its own Home Farm, where they produce meat, eggs and other organic food. Visitors can learn about the livestock, take part in feeding events, groom donkeys, go on a carriage ride pulled by shire horses and witness the live lambing (during April and May). There is a great adventure playground for kids, and the restaurant and cafés serve locally sourced produce.

The estate's mansion and other buildings are set in 18th century grounds, including a walled garden and parterre. There are some wonderful walks with stunning views of the open parkland, ancient woodland belts and a folly (sham ruins) in the shape of a ruined gothic castle. If you visit during September or October, the horse chestnut trees in front of the folly are where you can find the biggest and shiniest conkers.

29. Go wild at the Zoo

There are three zoos near Cambridge, the closest being Linton Zoo and Shepreth Wildlife Park.

Linton Zoo is a firm favourite with locals and has been here since 1972 as a family-run wildlife breeding centre for endangered species. This intimate zoo houses lots of different animals in its natural-looking enclosures, including giant tortoises, toucans, snow leopards, tigers, lions, zebra, tapir, reptiles and spiders. Keep an eye out for the dinosaurs dotted around and bring suitable footwear if it has been raining - the trails can get pretty muddy in wet weather.

There is something for everyone at Shepreth Wildlife Park, especially kids. Beginning in the mid '80s as Willers Mill Animal Sanctuary for injured and orphaned animals, the park has grown to house over a hundred different species including owls, meerkats, tigers, lemurs, red pandas, monkeys, maned wolves, coatis, otters and macaws. They have an on-site hedgehog hospital, a nocturnal house with bats, a tropical house with caimans and a Discovery Centre containing animal-related specimens. There is also a large adventure playground, an indoor play barn and a small Safari Train ride.

If you are willing to go a bit further afield, Hamerton Zoo Park near Sawtry is less than an hour's drive from Cambridge. With twenty acres of parkland, Hamerton is home to a huge variety of exotic animals and birds including cheetahs, tigers, small cats, maned wolves, corsac foxes, aardwolves, bintarongs, howler monkeys, gibbons, cassowaries, kookaburras, camels, snakes and reptiles. They also have domestic animals, such as goats and donkeys, some of which you are allowed to feed with food from special feeding stations. As well as the animals, Hamerton Zoo has great picnic and play areas, and a Railroad Train when the weather is dry.

Not far from St Ives, on the road to Somersham, is a wonderful conservation centre called The Raptor Foundation. Committed to rescuing and rehabilitating birds of prey and returning them to the wild, the Raptor Foundation offers the opportunity to meet, handle and learn about a variety of different birds, such as hawks, owls, kestrels and falcons. They also have flying displays here.

30. Walk the Devil's Dyke

To the north of the city between Cambridge and Newmarket lies Devil's Dyke, the finest anglo-saxon earthwork of its kind in Britain. This defensive earth bank with its steep ditch runs in a straight line for over seven miles and is a popular walking route.

Starting at the car park of the Dyke's End pub in the village of Reach, admire beautiful views of the open countryside as you walk along the top of Devil's Dyke before coming down off it and crossing the fields to Swaffham village, which has two windmills. Follow the track back towards Reach and then finish up with a drink back at the pub. Wildflowers, birds and butterflies make the trail even lovelier in summer.

And the name? Well, local legend has it that the devil himself came to a nearby wedding uninvited, and when the guests tried to chase him away he stormed off in anger, leaving a groove in the land with his fiery tail.

31. Grab a Bargain at a Car Boot Sale

Car boot sales have become as much a British institution as the Royal Family and are a great place to grab a bargain. OK, so a lot of it is just junk, but they really are good fun, and you know what they say - one man's trash is another man's treasure. There are several to choose from in Cambridge and most charge a very small admission fee.

Trumpington Road Park & Ride on the outskirts of the city holds a car boot sale throughout the year on Sundays and is open to buyers from 6.30am. Brampton Racecourse car boot sale near Huntingdon is also on Sundays (except on race days) and open from 9am.There is a market and car boot sale held at Oakington Business Park every Saturday from 7am. Burgess Hall in St Ives has an indoor car boot sale on selected dates throughout the year, open to buyers from 8am.

Top tips:

- If you don't want to end up with arms full of unwanted junk, have some idea of what you're looking for before you go and try not to be distracted.
- Pop a plastic bag (or two) in your pocket. You'll need it to carry your bargains home in.
- Get there early, when the best bargains are to be had.
- Haggle. You might be surprised how low some sellers are willing to go to get rid of it.

32. Discover Denny Abbey's Ancient Ruins

The line between town and countryside remains more blurred in Cambridge than in any other city I have come across, so it makes sense that there would be a museum featuring aspects of Cambridgeshire rural life. With equipment and machinery on display, a 19th century fenman's hut, and a farmworker's cottage decked out to show how it might have looked in the 1940s, Denny Abbey Farmland Museum provides a brilliant insight into the way farming has changed over the years.

What makes this museum even more fascinating (and spooky) is that the Abbey here was founded in 1159 as a Benedictine monastery, then later used as a home for aged and infirm members of the Knights Templar. In 1308 it became a Franciscan nunnery, was dissolved by Henry VIII two centuries later and then used as a farm up until the 1960s. The museum and abbey are located just outside Waterbeach on the A10 towards Ely.

33. Explore Wandlebury and the Gog Magogs

To the south of Cambridge, atop an area of low chalk hills named the Gog Magogs, lies Wandlebury Country Park. Home to Wandlebury Ring, an Iron Age hill fort, the Gog Magogs are shrouded in mystery and local folklore. Depending on which tale you believe, the hills are either named after two giants called Gog and Magog who were buried here or one giant called Gogmagog, whose horse left a footprint in a chalkpit nearby. Some even claim Gog and Magog were gods rather than giants.

Gervase of Tilbury, author of the 13th century encyclopedic work Otia Imperialia, told of a fearsome warrior on horseback who would appear by moonlight to potential challengers if they went to the entrance of the fort and shouted out, "Knight to knight. Come forth!" After hearing stories of a Wandlebury giant observed from the nearby village of Sawston, archaeologist T. C. Letheridge became convinced of the existence of an ancient hill figure cut into the chalk here and in 1955 he began excavating Wandlebury hillside. He believed there was a link between the hill figure and Tilbury's moonlit warrior.

Letheridge's work revealed three figures, which he claimed dated to around 200 BC: a female warrior riding a chariot, a huge warrior wielding a sword and a sun-god. In 1957 he published a book called Gogmagog: The Buried Gods, but his findings have since been discredited due to his unconventional methods and lack of firm evidence.

Whatever the truth, Wandlebury and the Gog Magogs have a fascinating history. Today, the country park is a peaceful retreat for walkers and nature lovers, and the circular earthwork of the ancient hill fort can still be seen and walked along.

34. Tee up for a Round of Golf

"To find a man's true character, play golf with him." -

P. G. Wodehouse

According to a recent survey, Cambridge is the second driest place in the UK. Not only is that something to be incredibly proud of in a country synonymous with rainy days, but it's also great news for golfers.

There are several golf clubs in and around the city, the best of which is the Gog Magog Golf Club in Great Shelford, which has two very different 18-hole courses. Its Old Course has a long history (it was officially founded in 1901) and plenty of challenging elevations, as well as wonderful views across the Cambridgeshire countryside, while the newer Wandlebury Course has hosted regional qualifying for The Open for several years. Although not cheap, Gog Magog is well worth the money if you are an avid golfer.

For beginners, Cambridge Lakes Golf Course on Trumpington Road is a good place to start. A 9-hole par-3 course near to the city centre, it is reasonably priced with friendly and helpful staff.

Girton Golf Club on the outskirts of Cambridge is set in lovely parkland and extremely well maintained. It is flat, though challenging, with great greens.

35. Cheer on Cambridge United FC

Seeing as Cambridge is the birthplace of the rules of football, it's only fitting you should catch a match while you're here. Cambridge United play their home games at the Abbey Stadium on Newmarket Road, a couple of miles from the city centre.

A lower-league team with a loyal following dubbed the 'Amber Army', the U's are well worth seeing in action, as is their mascot Marvin the Moose. Just be prepared to hate Peterborough - they're our biggest rivals!

36. Visit two Special Cemeteries

A cemetery isn't usually the kind of place most of us would choose to hang out in, but there are two in Cambridge that each have something particularly unique to offer.

One I discovered purely by accident when I was looking for a shortcut between Huntingdon Road and Madingley Road. A short walk down All Souls Lane brings you to the Ascension Parish Burial Ground, where a notice at the entrance explains its history. Opened in 1869, the burial ground is the final resting place of various famous poets, historians, engineers, scientists and philosophers, including Ludwig Wittgenstein (considered to be one of the greatest philosophers of the 20th century) and Sir John Cockcroft (who split the atom in 1932). The cemetery itself is a quiet oasis of yew trees and pines - the perfect place to reflect on great minds of the past who helped shape our world today.

When the US entered the Second World War in December of 1941, it was the beginning of a 'friendly invasion' that brought more than three million Americans to Britain as part of their huge contribution to the Allies' offensive against Nazi-occupied Europe. They left a lasting legacy, influencing the culture of Britain and establishing a transatlantic friendship that is still strong today. The Cambridge American Cemetery and Memorial in Madingley Road is a permanent reminder of America's sacrifice and the only one of its kind in the UK. Here, there are nearly four thousand crosses marking the graves of men and women who gave their lives, as well as a Wall of the Missing inscribed with over five thousand names. It is a truly humbling place to visit.

37. Follow a Sculpture Trail

A great way to see the city while taking in a bit of modern art is to follow one of the walks set out by Cambridge Sculpture Trails. You can choose from three easy-to-follow trails which will guide you to over 70 different modern sculpture sites. Many of these 20th and 21st century works are located in college grounds, and Jesus College alone has a permanent collection of 16 sculptures.

Trail 1 takes approximately two hours and begins up near the railway station - perfect for combining with a trip to the Botanic Garden.

Trail 2 is the best option if you are planning on stopping en route for coffee or lunch, as it is based more around the city centre where there are plenty of restaurants and cafés.

Trail 3 begins at Churchill College and ends at the Isaac Newton Institute, taking in several college gardens along the way. It is further from the city centre and therefore a more quiet and peaceful option.

You can pick up a free map of all three trails from the tourist information centre at the Guildhall.

38. Go Retro at the Centre for Computing History

"Personal computers have become the most empowering tool we've ever created..." –

Bill Gates

Just over the railway bridge on Coldham's Lane, there is a left-hand turn that doubles back onto a commercial trading estate filled with electrical wholesalers, tile shops and auto part stores. Follow this road almost to the level crossing and you will find a hidden gem called the Centre for Computing History.

Established as an educational charity exploring the impact of developments in computing technology over the years, this is a fantastic hands-on museum that really gets you thinking about how technology has influenced the way we live today. The collection includes vintage computers, artefacts and memorabilia, and there are various gaming consoles and retro arcade machines set up for you to play on. It's a fun and educational trip down memory lane, especially the '80s classroom, and the mega processor on display is very impressive.

39. Learn About the life of Oliver Cromwell

Oliver Cromwell, one of England's most famous and controversial military figures, was born in the nearby town of Huntingdon in 1599 and attended Sidney Sussex College in Cambridge. He lived in and around the city for several years before joining the Parliamentarians during the English Civil War and eventually signing the order for the execution of King Charles I, leaving England without a monarch for the first time in history. He served as Lord Protector for a short while until his death in 1658.

Oliver Cromwell's family home near the cathedral in Ely has an exhibition about the Civil War and 17th century rooms recreating domestic life of that era. Other than Hampton Court Palace in London, it is the only one of his residences remaining.

He also lived in St Ives for several years and there is a statue of him in the market square here. Two of the arches of the town bridge had to be rebuilt after Cromwell destroyed them to prevent Charles I's troops from crossing.

Two years after Cromwell died, under the orders of King Charles II, those responsible for Charles I's death were hunted down and killed. Cromwell's body was dug up at Westminster, hanged and beheaded. There are varying accounts of what happened to his head, including tales of it being sold to a Swiss-French collector, but it was finally laid to rest in a secret location in the grounds of Sidney Sussex College.

There is also a museum about Cromwell's life in the centre of Huntingdon, located in the former Grammar School building where he attended as a boy.

40. Take part in a Live-action Puzzle Adventure

As well as being a museum, the aforementioned Oliver Cromwell's House at Ely has become part of the latest craze in live-action entertainment. Escape rooms are a popular activity for those wanting to try something different, and there is more than one to choose from in Cambridge.

The latest scenario at Oliver Cromwell's House is a lock-in at the Cromwell Arms, where the assistance of you and up to eight friends is required to prevent the murder of Queen Victoria. You will be greeted by a host in costume and given 60 minutes to solve the puzzles in order to accomplish your mission.

Lockhouse Escape Games, located in Cambridge's Regent Street, have three different scenarios each lasting around an hour. Stop a meteor from hitting Earth, escape an Egyptian tomb or pretend you're a secret agent from the Cold War era - the choice is yours.

Cambridge Escape Rooms off Cherry Hinton Road also have three immersive rooms for teams of up to six: Secret Of The Tomb, Heaven And Hell and The Bomb.

If you want to take part in something challenging and a little offbeat, this may be the perfect opportunity. Just keep your wits about you.

41. Celebrate the Written Word

"There is more treasure in books than in all the pirate's loot on Treasure Island."

\- Walt Disney

A university town wouldn't be complete without plenty of bookshops and Cambridge is no different. The city is home to the oldest publishing house in the world, Cambridge University Press. It originated from the Letters Patent granted to the University by Henry VIII in 1534 and has grown to become a renowned global publisher of academic and research journals with more than 50 offices around the world. Their Cambridge shop is on the oldest bookshop site in the country, located on the corner of Trinity Street and St Mary's Street in the city centre.

If you're a bookworm or you just love the unmistakable musky smell of old books, head to St Edward's Passage where there are two bookshops - G. David and The Haunted Bookshop - selling antiquarian and secondhand books. The Haunted Bookshop is a good place to hunt for first editions and this small shop has a surprisingly large collection, including a great selection of children's books. As well as selling bargain books, G. David sell maps, prints and engravings.

The Cambridge Literary Festival is held twice yearly in and around Cambridge and is a celebration of the power of the written word in all its forms, for writers as well as readers. It showcases the best in contemporary fiction, with workshops for adults and an extensive programme of activities for young people and children to nurture their creativity and enthusiasm. Past guest speakers have included Ian Rankin, Dawn French, Ian McEwan, Roger McGough, Andrew Motion, Celia Imrie, Germaine Greer and Cressida Cowell.

42. Learn to Paddleboard at Milton Country Park

After all that punting you've been doing, paddleboarding should be a breeze. If you fancy having a go at one of the world's fastest-growing sports, the British Standup Paddleboarding Association operates coaching and sessions for complete beginners or those with more experience at Milton Country Park from May to September.

Located just north of Cambridge, tranquil Milton Country Park is a lovely place where you can walk and cycle in woodland and lake surroundings. The park is managed by the Cambridge Sport Lakes Trust, and there are other regular sporting activities and events on offer too. Easy to learn and lots of fun; what's not to love?

43. Satisfy your Sweet Tooth

A room lined from floor to ceiling with shelves of humongous glass jars full of stripy humbugs, powdery jelly babies and luminous lollipops; that is how a traditional English sweet shop should look. If you've got a bit of a sweet tooth, your first stop should be Hardy's Original Sweet Shop on the corner of St John's Street opposite the

Round Church. Mr Simms' Olde Sweet Shoppe on King's Parade stocks all the old favourites plus a few new ones.

If it's chocolate you're after, Bellina Chocolate House on Bridge Street sells the most divine handmade truffles I've ever tasted. Chocolat Chocolat on St Andrews Street is famous for its handmade sheet chocolate, crafted in a unique French style and combined with lots of different interesting flavours like French sea salt and freeze dried raspberries. They also sell hot chocolate and ice cream.

Over on King's Parade, opposite King's College, the Fudge Kitchen crafts my favourite sweet treat. For smooth and creamy fudge in a variety of delicious flavours, plus fudge sauces and hot fudge, this place really is the best.

44. Ride the Miniature Railway at Audley End

If you join the B1383 near Ickleton and drive on past the village of Littlebury, you will come to a break in the trees on your left that provides one of my favourite views in England. There - with its lovely lawns laid out before the River Cam - stands Audley End House, one of the finest Jacobean houses in England. Audley End is cared for by English Heritage, and you can explore its magnificent staterooms, take a stroll through the formal gardens and learn all about Victorian England in its 1880s Wing.

On the other side of the road from the mansion is a little gem of a place and a very special experience for families: the Audley End Miniature Railway. Mini steam and diesel engines offer rides through the pretty country estate woodland, which was designed by Capability Brown and is home to lots of wildlife.

As you pootle along, you will see hundreds of teddy bears hidden in the trees or having secret picnics, and if you come during special events at Christmas or Easter you might even be treated to a performance in the middle of the woods. We went at Easter and the train was halted by the Easter Bunny, who gave everyone chocolate eggs.

As well as the trains there is an Enchanted Fairy and Elf walk complete with tiny wooden tree houses, a café serving hot and cold food, and a large picnic and play area.

45. Catch a show at the Arts or ADC

Many famous actors and actresses cut their acting teeth while studying at the University of Cambridge, including Emma Thompson, Rachel Weisz, Ian McKellan, John Cleese, Stephen Fry and Rowan Atkinson. The city's world-famous Footlights drama group still performs plays and sketch shows, and you can catch their hilarious Smokers show at the ADC Theatre on Park Street every fortnight.

The ADC is run almost entirely by students of the University and has a varied programme including musicals, adaptations and Shakespearean favourites. Owned by Corpus Christi College and managed by the ADC, the Corpus Playroom at St Edward's Passage is home to the Fletcher Players drama company and is a more intimate venue for fringe productions.

For bigger productions and touring shows, try the Arts Theatre. I'm a big fan of their annual pantomime and I've also seen a variety of performances here, including The Woman In Black, West Side Story and Anything Goes.

If you like stand-up comedy, Cambridge Corn Exchange gets some pretty big names. I have been to see Jimmy Carr, Henning Wehn and Jon Richardson here and tickets were very reasonably priced.

46. See Lord Fairhaven's Collections

Formerly a 13th century priory, Anglesey Abbey is a country house owned by the National Trust and located in the village of Lode, just north of the city. There are over a hundred acres of beautiful gardens here displaying an impressive array of plants and statuary collected by previous owner Lord Fairhaven, who was very wealthy.

Some of his vast collection of paintings, clocks and antiques is on display inside the house, but the gardens are simply not to be missed. In particular, the Abbey's snowdrop festival is a huge draw, with more than 300 varieties flowering here in late winter. Tree-lined avenues, numerous plant species and a working watermill make wandering through the grounds here seem like a dream.

47. Get Hands-on at the Science Festival

Every year in March or April, talks, workshops and exhibitions covering subjects from astronomy to zoology take place across the city as part of the Cambridge Science Festival. Giving an insight into a whole range of scientific topics, the festival provides a brilliant opportunity to discuss and explore issues related to science in the ever-changing and developing world we live in.

There are hundreds of events to attend and most are free of charge. This year's programme included talks on gene editing and the science of ice cream; hands-on workshops about volcanic rocks and roaming robots; and shows about the extinction of the dinosaurs and the importance of bees. If you want to try and make some sense of the world, this is the place to start.

48. Eat and Drink at Bun Shops, Bars and Bistros

"One cannot think well, love well, sleep well, if one has not dined well."

- Virginia Woolf, A Room of One's Own

Cambridge boasts such a variety of great places to eat and drink, with something to suit everyone. I have tried to narrow it down to just a few of my favourites, but you're bound to discover more if you wander around its quaint and charming streets.

Actor Stephen Fry famously raved about the Chelsea buns at Fitzbillies on Trumpington Street and with good reason. This bakery and café has been serving its cake and pastry delights to students and locals since 1920, and they really are the best.

Not far from Fitzbillies, on the corner of Bene't Street, Aromi is a great little place for coffee and cake, serving up tasty and authentic Italian treats at a reasonable price.

Situated inside St Michael's Church, the Michaelhouse Café does some lovely light lunches. Its convenient location close to the colleges and tranquil, welcoming atmosphere make it one of my top picks.

If you are veggie or vegan, the Rainbow Café on King's Parade has a delicious and varied menu. It is situated down an alleyway in a basement, so is small but cosy, and the staff are very efficient. Also, try Stem and Glory on King's Street or Mitcham's Corner, where they have a wide selection of vegan lunches, snacks and cakes to eat in or take away.

If you're looking for somewhere more upmarket, there are a number of fine-dining restaurants in Cambridge. Midsummer House is the very best of these, with an á la carte menu, white tablecloths and an elegant conservatory location next to the river.

For great service and tasty, well-presented food, head for Trinity on Trinity Street or its sister restaurant Varsity on St Andrew's Street. Varsity's rooftop bar provides spectacular views across the city.

De Luca Cucina & Bar on Regent Street is a must on a Friday or Saturday night, with delicious Italian food, a lively atmosphere and an upstairs cocktail bar with piano singer.

Finally, for a late-night snack after a night out on the town, Greek take-away The Gardenia on Rose Crescent really hits the spot.

49. Get Around like a Local

There are several main car parks close to the city centre: the Grand Arcade, Park Street, Grafton East and Grafton West, Queen Anne Terrace and Castle Hill. While there is no getting around the fact that parking in Cambridge is expensive, there are other options.

If you are arriving by car, the city's Park & Ride service has five different sites on the outskirts of Cambridge and is colour coded for ease of use:

Blue = Trumpington Park & Ride
Green = Babraham Road Park & Ride
Orange = Newmarket Road Park & Ride
Purple = Milton Park & Ride
Red = Madingley Park & Ride

Park & Ride buses depart every 10 minutes on Monday to Saturday (20 minutes after 6.30pm) and every 15 minutes on Sunday (9am-6pm). All services stop in the city centre, and the Newmarket Road and Milton buses also stop at the Grafton interchange.

The guided busway connects Cambridge with St Ives and Huntingdon, and is fast and convenient. You can pick it up from the city centre.

If you want the proper tourist experience, City Sightseeing offers a hop-on hop-off bus service which stops at all the city's major attractions and gives information in nine different languages. Departing every 40 minutes, a complete tour takes about 1 hour 20 minutes and can be combined with a punt trip.

Arriving by train? The railway station is a bit of a walk from the centre, but buses are available to take you there. You might also want to consider getting a PlusBus ticket, which will give you unlimited bus travel around Cambridge. Trains run frequently from Cambridge to London King's Cross and London Liverpool Street, Peterborough, Ipswich, Ely and Norwich, as well as a service to Stansted Airport.

Cambridge is the cycling capital of the UK and one of the best and safest cities for exploring by bike. There is an extensive network of cycle lanes and routes for you to enjoy, plus free designated cycle parks at Park Street and the Grand Arcade. Bike hire is available from various places across the city, including City Cycle Hire, Rutland Cycling and Cambridge Bike Tours.

Having a car makes visiting some of the surrounding attractions a lot easier, but you won't need it in the city centre, as Cambridge is such a compact and walkable city. Instead, do what the locals do and get around by bus, bike or on foot.

50. Book the Perfect Accommodation

Cambridge has a great range of accommodation options, from boutique hotels to less expensive guest houses and apartments, and closer doesn't necessarily have to mean costlier if you're willing to go self-catering.

The Student Castle aparthotel is great value and a short walk away from the city centre across Jesus Green. An apartment at Gwydir Street House is slightly more expensive, but has free parking available nearby.

If you are looking for luxury accommodation, both the Varsity Hotel & Spa and the Hotel du Vin & Bistro provide oodles of cocktails and class, each with their own elegant restaurant and bar.

More family-friendly options close to the city centre include the Premier Inn on Newmarket Road and the Holiday Inn Express off Coldham's Lane.

If you have a car, you could always stay just outside Cambridge and take advantage of the Park & Ride service. The Holiday Inn near Impington, Hallmark Hotel at Bar Hill, Cambridge Belfry at Cambourne and Quy Mill Hotel & Spa are all within a half-hour drive from the city.

For those looking to really experience the city's academic history, you can even stay in college accommodation during student vacations. With single and twin options and ensuites available, it is certainly a unique and interesting alternative.

Top Reasons to book this Trip

- Heritage and history. Cambridge is old and there has been a town here since Roman times.

- Stimulation for the mind. Surely being in the company of nobel prize winners and academic heroes is bound to give your brain a boost?

- Chelsea buns. Sticky, crammed with yummy currants and thoroughly English.

- The royal connection. To mark their marriage, Britain's favourite royal couple, William and Kate, became Duke and Duchess of Cambridge.

- The first official game of football was held here.

- You might spot one of the Cambridge Night Climbers, a group of students who scale the college buildings at night and have been the subject of several books.

- The weather. Cambridge is the second driest city in the UK after the capital.

Jennifer Baines

> TOURIST
GREATER THAN A TOURIST

Visit GreaterThanATourist.com:
http://GreaterThanATourist.com

Sign up for the Greater Than a Tourist Newsletter:
http://eepurl.com/cxspyf

Follow us on Facebook:
https://www.facebook.com/GreaterThanATourist

Follow us on Pinterest:
http://pinterest.com/GreaterThanATourist

Follow us on Instagram:
http://Instagram.com/GreaterThanATourist

Follow on Twitter:
http://twitter.com/ThanaTourist

Jennifer Baines

> TOURIST
GREATER THAN A TOURIST

Please leave your honest review of this book on Amazon and Goodreads. Thank you. We appreciate your positive and constructive feedback. Thank you.

Jennifer Baines

NOTES

Made in the USA
Middletown, DE
11 December 2020